A Wisewoman's Book of Tea Leaf Reading

Written By Pat Barki
illustrated by Hermione Heritage

The Wise Woman's Wisdom Series

www.capallbann.co.uk

A Wisewoman's Book of Tea Leaf Reading

©Copyright Pat Barki 2004
Illustrations ©Copyright Hermione Heritage

ISBN 186163 166 9

Cover design by Paul Mason
Internal and cover illustrations by Hermione Heritage

Published by:

Capall Bann Publishing
Auton Farm
Milverton
Somerset
TA4 1NE

Acknowledgments

For all those who seek to know, and for the wisdom of the old ones

For Amber Rose, my beautiful Granddaughter, to whom the knowledge is now passed - love to you sweetheart

For Lauren Dye, for being, whose love, friendship and sisterhood knows no limits and from whose heart shines the light of grace

My family, for their patience and presence always.

P. B.

With thanks and love to all my family for their encouragement and patience and to the magical landscape of the West Country for inspiration

H. H.

Contents

Foreword

In the modern western world, many of the older, traditi-onal methods of divination are being revived as people are realising the need for such guidance to cope with the ever increasing stresses of everyday life. Through the teachings of the Old Religion's method of tea leaf reading, you will learn how a Wise Woman's method of tea leaf reading is different from the other methods of divination.

Wise folk use a magical method in order keep order and control over the energies that are present during a reading. What follows here is an explanation of the method handed down to me, and brought down the years from generation to generation of wise women in my family.

The method that is set out in this book has been handed down in my family, I know that it was tried and tested over many years, so you may now benefit from that experience and you may even feel like you are becoming part of the ancient tradition. If it suits you to use it, please do so, but do not follow my methods laid out blindly or without thought. Let your own spirit lead you as you become more confident and allow your own experience to build your skill.

Once you relax you will feel the broader inter-pretations of the symbols coming to you. You will learn what the patterns and combination will mean. I have constructed and included an index in the back of the book and these are as concise as possible in their individual meaning. If you get two or more together write down the meanings on a sheet of paper and see what conclusions you can draw. If you have properly prepared yourself for the reading, it will come to you quite easily. Go with your intuition, as it is your greatest asset in divining the energy in the tea cup

When you read this book, you will find that there will be no references to other books at the end as none were consulted. The material for this book is written as it has been passed down through my family and now it is being lovingly passed on to you.

I ask you to guard this wisdom, use it wisely and carefully as you are working with the forces of life and they are to be respected. These are the forces that have helped us to survive through the ages. They are not for party games or for monetary gain. Most Wise Women do ask a nominal fee for a reading, that represents an exchange of energy. This is why a fee should never be exaggerated. In other words, we feel that people have to go out and spend their life energy to get the money so it becomes an exchange of energy, thus forming a balance.

Wise Women also believe that when a predicted major life event comes to pass that you must cross her palm with a piece of silver. Now in today's world our coins are not silver but if you give her a 50p piece that will do the trick. It will bring good luck and fortune to you

So Mote it Be
Pat Barki, 2003

Section One

HOW IT ALL BEGAN

When I was a young girl, I learned the arts of the old religion from my father and also from my adored grandmother. When I was with her, I would especially love to have my teacup read. Despite her resistance to read my tea cup all the time, I would pester her until she gave in. With great anticipation I would carefully strain the excess tea off through my teeth, swish it around three times and up-end it in my saucer.

I must explain that the reason Nana was resistant to my pleadings at first this is due to an "unwritten law" of the old religion that one should never read for oneself. Additionally, it is hard to be asked to read for one's loved ones as they are close to the heart, and telling the (unhappy) truth, should there be any, may be very hard (although I believe that unhappy news should be given by a loved one). This is why giving readings for family and close friends is not a good idea (but it is not against any hard fast 'rules' of the old ways or religion).

As an illustration of how serious this is I want to tell the following story. Some time ago, one of my best friends was deeply in love with a man from abroad. She

was living in America and he in Europe. She believed that he truly loved her and that on her next visit she was convinced he would ask her to marry him. She asked me to read from her tea-cup and tell her what she could expect.

It was so hard telling her that I did not see a ring or a marriage to this man in the tea cup. I did remind her that these images were shadows and could possibly be changed with foreknowledge of other things. I knew from the reading that he would not marry her. It was a difficult thing for me to have to tell her but later she said she was glad to have had the reality check from me, rather than from a stranger, or find out the cold reality when she went to visit him. She settled down as a result of the reading and was not surprised when he did not propose, they ultimately became good friends and have kept in touch. These events are always good lessons for me.

There was always the smell of fresh herbs in my Nana's house and it felt like a haven away from the harsh world. In this wonderful space I felt secure and warm, able to concentrate on what I wanted to know about the energy around me. I would sit on the floor beside her chair, next to the fireplace with her broom and wonderful collection of staffs and rocks she had collected over the years. Nana would stare into the cup, turning it and studying it with great concentration. Sometimes she would smile because she could guess the question I asked by the way the leaves had formed various patterns and would, simply say to me, " you are in such a hurry, half the fun in life is waiting to find out, put your trust in the Universe

that everything will come round as it should". Try telling this to a moonstruck 17 year old!

Seeing the eager anticipation in my eyes she would dutifully and deftly read the symbols in my tea cup, and would offer me the time old interpretations. We would discuss how this could effect my life and what they would mean in the scope of what I was attempting to do at the time. These discussions are important because they help expand on what is given and helps with understanding one's life in a better way. I wrote everything down and studied my notes afterwards. This oracle did help me get through many things as it helped to give me confidence and patience while waiting for the universe to turn. It was the greatest gift I could give myself.

History in the Brewing

My Nana said that reading tea leaves from a cup with the black tea used today probably originated in the regions of the world wherever tea is naturally grown, such as India, Sri Lanka, Kenya, and China. Reading the leaves of the tea we know today only took hold in Britain when shipments of tea from around the world began to arrive in the tall ships and it was discovered that tea was for making a beverage not for making a form of porridge, as some seventeenth century people thought. Nana told me that tea was first brought to the Europe by the Dutch. The problem for the tea importers in the beginning was that it took so long to get the tea to port that much of the tea would have rotted in the ships hold. In order to solve this problem ships were built for speed so that the journey time was shortened. Today these are known as the clipper ships and they race at various times and places around the world still today.

Another interesting point was that rewards were given to the first ship to enter the port of one hundred guineas which started the tea competitions. The East Indian Trading Company became the most widely known.

Nana told me that before this time the ancient Britons must have developed the arts of leaf reading with teas made of herbs and plant barks and leaves as the science of herbal use began with these early people. They more than likely noticed that after they drank the liquid patterns would form and that these forms represented animals and other things that had their own character or energies as we know them. In other words, then, while tea leaf reading as we know it today may be only a recent historical development, it is likely that the principles come from a much older tradition. There is a good likelihood that the arts of tea leaf reading evolved from the observation of plant and leaf energies by ancient peoples. Today's art is therefore the result of a collective knowledge through the ages.

When I talk about this collective knowledge, I mean the experiences of life and survival techniques that have come to include the forms of divination, including leaf reading. This is shown in how those wise folk who lived on the earth before us left behind traces of themselves and how they lived. All around us there are wonderful clues in the ancient historical sites and monuments as to where the knowledge we have today came from.

Learned Wisdom

Much of the old history and wisdom is passed to us in a verbal form. Since many of the early observations came about before printed language like books. One of the lessons of prediction may have started with simple under-standings and observation which is demon-strated in the way our ancestors learned to forecast or predict or divine the weather. They did this by observing the energies of nature in the world around, above, and below them; sometimes by listening to the wind in the trees and also observing how, under certain conditions it would alter the natural position of the leaves. They knew, we have been told, for example, that when the leaves of a tree showed their underside that a serious storm was brewing. If the leaves only rustled it may not be as bad.

Another was to watch the behaviour of livestock, if they huddled together under a tree it was bad, if they laid down in a huddle under a tree it would be very bad weather. It was therefore discovered that natural energy forces could alert us to incoming conditions. Now with regard to tea leaf reading it is this same type of method being used. We use human energy to discover what lie's within our own path or that which is incoming in order to prepare and make the best out of each situation in our lives.

The Human Energy and Collective Wisdom

In addition to how collective knowledge about natural energy forces in the world outside the human body was understood, it was observed that the human body had regular correspondences to nature as well. Women menstruate by the moon cycle and many in correspondence to the direct pattern. This is because there is a connection between that which is inside the human body and the outer world. The human energy emanates from the inner part of the being, some call it the spirit or soul and spreads outward.

In each area of the body, there are energy emission points and those are a person's natural magnetic poles. This energy circles around the body in what appears to be layers. Some cultures, such as the people in India, call these layers, Aura, and the magnetic poles chakras. It is very different from person to person and can be altered by health and circumstance. In addition, this energy has imprinted onto it all the information about that inner being or ethos. The information each person carries is that which has been gathered and imprinted from other journeys on earth. Events that happen to a person during this time on earth is added to that past imprinting to make up the person's collective ethos and wisdom. This is what that person's natural forces consist of. It is this natural force then that outwardly effects the tea leaves manifesting the information contained in the energy into a readable pattern. From these patterns, the aspects of future events can reason-ably be calculated.

In other words, the energy of a person manifest into physical patterns and will attract certain patterns and images, which in this case, causes the leaves in the teacup to form patterns. In essence, these natural forces take the energy that is invisible to the naked eye and make it visible. Again, through careful study and observation, we can predict with a fair amount of accuracy the likelihood of events in the future, like the leaves and the storms.

Wisdom of Imprinting

Because imprinting is the source of the information that is either on your inner bands of energy or will be, I want to explain this process to you in greater detail. While this may seem rather distant from the subject of tea leaf reading it really is at its very centre. Unless you have an in-depth understanding of that which causes patterns to form you will not understand the relationship of many patterns to the person you are working with. For the purposes of this book, rather than others of its kind, understanding ethos is what makes the way in which Wise Women understand and practice the arts of divination different from others. Wise Women examine the source and the "cause and effect" relationship in someone's life and therefore is called natural magic.

Let us do a simple exercise. You know what an apple is. You know what it feels like, you know what it tastes like, you know its shapes, its colour etc. Even when you do not have a real physical apple in front of you, you can still picture an apple in your head.

This is because the energy of the apple's properties has been imprinted or transferred into the energy of your thoughts. Now, you do not have to think of an apple all the time to know that the information about an apple is there, you can summon that image into your mind whenever you want to or at the suggestion of the word. Divination produces or summons images that are imprinted in our energies that are around us.

People have paths that they are meant to follow which has its direction formulated in their natural energy but is affected by the events that happen in their lives. While sometime humans think they know what is best, they often settle for second or third best through sheer ignorance of what their true capabilities are. This is what divination is meant to help with.

Therefore, when a person picks up a teacup and drinks from it, it is in the handling of the cup, that causes the transferring of one's energies to the cup, liquid and eventually the leaf fragments in the bottom of the cup.

In turn, when one has drunk the liquid and turned the cup, the energy forms or manifests patterns of what is contained in the person's energies. From there, it is a careful study to understand the patterns and how they may pertain to that person's life.

If it is a question that is to be answered and that question has been thought of during the drinking of the liquid, often the direction to take appears at the bottom of the cup. Sometimes there are factors that may delay a response and appear in a later reading. You will be able to tell this because the answer will feel and even look incomplete. The forces of life have a great timetable and we cannot force it no matter how much we want to. When the time for us to know things is at hand we will know, but not before that. This is where the old wise people have learned the wisdom of being patient and being still.

Generally, because divination as a practice has always been a means to figure out survival of some sort, it can cast light onto the shadows of the future so one can alter or prepare for them. If there is nothing in the cup than there is nothing to be concerned about at the moment. Many people express fear of what may lie ahead, but what lies ahead is already there and to have advance light on it can remove the fear and help us move ahead with confidence.

Sue

Another woman I did a reading for had come to me because she had just gotten out of a relationship with a very abusive and dark person. She was very afraid of him. She wanted to get out of the area as fast as possible but did not know where to go. This was the reason and question of her reading. I could see that getting rid of the old boy friend made way for the right person for her to enter her life. I told her that I could see in her tea cup no movement of home or job at all. She had a wonderful job that she really liked.

I asked her if there had been a new person come to the company from the Chicago area as I could see a map in the cup. In fact there had been. Alan was widowed and had lived in the area along time ago, having divorced an alcoholic wife he had moved to Chicago. His ex-wife had died, leaving a teenage son, Alan had moved back. I could see that they were so right for each other and the energy in the tea cup was leaping up and down in my hand. I told her to be patient and wait, that the man was in her periphery. She was unsure but agreed to give it six weeks.

Three months went by and I had another call from her. She was really excited, she and Alan were together and were really happy. I did a reading for Alan and the two cups matched up. They eventually got married and I went to their home to clear out any bad energy from the ex-wife. What would have happened if she had impulsively taken flight? There are more stories like this that demonstrate that fear of the unknown can cause us to act in an unwise manner. Divination has helped many people to make better choices.

The Leaves Today

In the 19th and 20th centuries, tea leaf reading became a social event, particularly in the Victorian era, during a time when many, mostly women, may have felt out of control or helpless before the rapid pace of life. Women, but sometimes men, frequented tea parlours or tea rooms, and had their cups read by the local wise woman. Perhaps this continued need and the socialization of tea leaf reading was in order to offer some sort of control over their lives when most women had no control.

As the laws that regulated women's lives changed and women were able to get more control over the events of their lives through education and job opportunities the use of divination for forecasting events became a mere amusing pastime. It is interesting to note that many of the wise women lived in villages that did not have such rigid levels of social distinctions and they had far more control over their lives. They had to work, and earn money.

In actual fact the use of divination is now re-emerging as many women of all social classes are realising that the information provided in forms of divination is more vital to them now than it ever was.

The stress of life today on the earth is causing much strife and confusion and getting back in touch with one's self and one's path in life can help make things more simple and life more enjoyable. Divination can help one avoid many of the pitfalls and prepare in ways that will help life be fuller and happier all around.

NOVELTY TEAPOTS FROM 1890 TO THE PRESENT DAY

24

How to Perform a Tea Leaf Reading

Why a Wisewoman's Way is Different

A wisewoman's method of reading tea leaves is different from the general methods of readings currently used. Wise women know how to charge the leaves with a magic wand and balance the energies, manifest the patterns and answers to the seeker's questions for the correctness and the good of all.

Why wisewomen feel this is important is that a harmon-ious balance is very important between the inner and outer self. When the energy from the inner self is brought into the conscious self, like the inform-ation about the apple, it is important that the transferring of this information be correct and complete so that a better situation for that person is realised. Wise women are very concerned with these balances because if their balances are not correct that is when dis-ease of mind or body can happen. I recommend that you try the method that will follow and see how it feels to you.

The Tea Reading Equipment

Pots and Cups

I have kept several wonderful old china teapots especially for the times when I do tealeaf reading. You should hunt around for just the one that feels right to you or you may have a family heirloom that you treasure. It is a good idea to keep this teapot just for doing readings so that it remains special and the energy is not contaminated. Store it away from the family dishes and tea pots as well. Give it a place in a quiet part of your home away from the usual household traffic.

Next, you will need some china teacups and saucers, the finer the bone china the better. Be warned that it is always important to warm your china cup in warm to hot water before pouring boiling hot liquid into it as it will crack. Like my teapots I have a special set of tea cups and saucers and cake plates for these occasions and make sure that you keep them as I have suggested for the tea pot. I usually offer a cookie or biscuit with the tea as it is very much part of the ritual. It doesn't matter if milk is added or not but a teaspoon of sugar is a basic requirement.

The Tea

Use a fine loose tea; in Britain Typhoo, a Darjeeling, is a good tea for reading or some of the better loose teas sold at tea merchants. Always use black teas, not green tea, for this purpose. Please use filtered or the purest water available. When boiling the water for tea use a real kettle and place it on the stove for a good, rolling boil and let the water boil for a minute. Use one spoonful for each cup and one for the pot, so for two people use three spoonfuls of tea. If possible, have all of the electric equipment off in the kitchen and do the boiling and brewing by candlelight, even if it is daytime.

Keep your tea in a tea caddy made out of natural material away from light and electric equipment. As a general rule I keep all my divination equipment well away from everything else in a special place in my house that is set aside for this purpose It is also good to have what I call an unpolluted space where your special things are kept and also that you have a place in your home where you can go some quiet time.

Wands

If you are to practice this method of teal leaf reading you will need a wand of your own. Yes, you can buy one commercially made but it will not give you the same results as if you gathered the stick and made it yourself.

Making a wand is simple. Every person has his or her own tree or wood. In the old Celtic ways the trees were associated with each of the seasons and are specific time periods like astrology. The magic of each tree is part of an alphabet, individual magical meanings which are associated then with your date of birth. So, if you really want to do a good job as part of your tools you will want to find the wood that is associated with your birth. (see page 45 of the index for a full explanation)

Go for a walk and find a tree that corresponds to your birthday or one that you like that bears fruit, such as the universal tree - Apple. Wisewomen always like oak or apple the best. When you enter the woodland look around to see if a suitable branch is on the ground already.

This branch needs to be about an inch to an inch and one half thick and about nine inches long. If there is one right there on the ground then pick it up and thank the tree for her gift. If not, ask the tree for one, look for a dead branch, never, ever take living wood. If there is not a branch on the ground then find another tree. Many times, I have asked the tree and a branch piece has fallen from aloft and answered my request. Always remember to thank the particular tree for her gift.

Getting Started

What Kind of Reading is Best?
You will first want to decide which reading is best for the situation at hand. There are two types of reading. The first type of reading is to present a cyclical reading that looks at (your) year to come. This will take into account each of the next coming seasons. If you are beginning a reading in the summer then the reader will look at the southerly position of your cup first as that is where you are beginning from and most relevant to you now. This is the reading most recommended for any first reading, whether it be the first reading you have ever had or the first reading with a new reader.

The second is seasonally specific in which the reader will draw in only that seasons energy when she or he charges the cup. This charge is given later on. This will look specifically where you are now and what are the immediate influences currently or likely to be active in your sphere.

Usually Wise Women only recommend one reading a cycle or every three months. Wise Women break the year into four phases as are the seasons.

Winter is the months of November, December and January. Spring is the months of February, March, and April. Summer is considered May, June, and July, with Autumn being the months of August, September, and October. Readings are always best if done in the first month of each season, after the new moon and before the full moon.

Finishing the Brew

Now your tea is in the pot brewing, use your lovingly made wand and draw energy down from the Father sky by holding the top end of your wand upward so that the other end is pointed downward. Now draw it up from the mother earth as the wand is also poised to draw from both directions. Now perform what is called charging the tea in the pot of water. What this does is empowers the brew to combine the energies of the God and the Goddess in perfect wisdom and prevents energies that would be untrue to effect your efforts. Place the point of your wand over the tea pot and make the sign of the pentacle as shown in the diagram.

This symbol represents the four directions as well as the elements, earth, water, fire and air. The fifth point means as above so below, or as in the great Universe so here on earth. It invokes the great spirit or soul. In essence, what invoking this symbol does is to bring into balance all the elements of life and draws energy from the earth and the sky or the heavenly bodies above us.

One suggestion for a charge that would look at the whole year to come might be:

I draw down the energy of the cosmos in all the most perfect aspects. I draw from the mother earth all her most perfect aspects. I ask that all energies positive and negative that would come to do harm be bound and banished. Leaves of life, we ask that you help us to understand the questions asked today and make clear that which is right and correct for her/him to know at this time. SO may it be forever.

Tynnaf i lawr egni'r bydysawd yn eu holl agweddau prffaith. Tynnaf o'r famddaear eu holl agweddau perffaith. Erfynnaf fod pob nerth sydd am achosi niwed yn cael ci atal. Dail bywd, gofynnaf am eich cymorth i'n helpu ni ddeall y pethe y mae .... wedi gofn heddiw, ac i egluro'r hyn sydd yn iawn. Felly y bydd, bendith arnom.

A seasonal one would include the name of the deity that is associated with the season that you are working in. It is Cerridwyn in the north or winter, Danu in the east or Spring, Arta in the south or summer, and Banba in the west for Autumn.

Beginning the Reading - Creating An Ambient Atmosphere

Mind expansion is the first step to getting a full and accurate reading. Most of us spend more of our waking hours in a state of negativity than we do in a positive state. When we do this, we cause the energies around us to cave in on our brains. This inhibits our ability to put out our energy into the universe or be a good receiver. This is why we feel stuck and confused about things. We need to learn to turn this around.

Before you go to a reading or perform one, try this exercise. Find a quiet private spot with as little external noise as possible. Light a white and a black candle and be peaceful. Imagine that you have a white band of light circling your head and right on the top of your head is a purple light that seems to come from your head itself. Now imagine that the white light lifting up and out from your head and going out several feet.

This may take some time to get this vision into your mind but keep trying until you manage it. You may have to do several sittings but that is OK just keep at it and don't tense up. Once you can see this light expanding, when it does get several feet from your head hold it in that position. Let the purple light flow in and fill in the expansion. This will relieve the pressure on your brain and inner being and will expand your reception as well as your ability to put out your good light.

Now you will be ready to be a good reader or a good listener. This exercise is a good one to do whenever you are feeling under pressure it will relieve it right away. Try and use it when negativity creeps in. Now, when beginning the reading. Both the reader and the questioner should sit quietly and the room be closed off.

The reader will light a candle preferably a black one, since black lets in the most light, and wisewomen believe that light carries wisdom, and asks that all that is done herein be for the correctness and good of all and that both reader and questioner be protected from all energies positive and negative that would come to do harm. This exercise is done in addition to charging the tea pot and brew as you need to charge the energy around the questioner and the reader.

Additionally this exercise ensures that the reading will be done in a balanced and protected environment. The reader will always conclude each charge with the phrase FELLY Y BYDEL to cast and bind the words.

Now, the reader will ask the questioner to breathe slowly while slowly drinking the tea and focusing on the burning candle. Concentrate on why this reading is desired and on any question that is being asked.

Once the liquid is drunk, sieve the last bit of liquid through your teeth as much as you can, leaving a few drops in the bottom, the equivalent of about half a teaspoon.

Hold the teacup handle firmly between the thumb and fingers of your right hand and turn the cup three times in a clockwise circular motion and then turn the cup upside down in the saucer. Let the cup rest in the saucer for a moment. Take a slow deep breath and tap the cup thrice or three times.

Turn the saucer clockwise until the handle is facing you. Lift the cup straight up do not turn it right side up yet, and look underneath to see if any liquid drips off quickly or if it takes a moment for a drop to fall. Then turn the cup right side up. If you are doing a full cycle reading the handle is in the south. If you are doing a specific seasonal reading then your cup will represent only the attributes of the season you are in.

The Wheel of the Year in Your Cup

With the handle downward

The North part of your cup represents the time before beginning it is the time when things lay in wait. It is the time of dreams for the future to be made from the protected realms. The Goddess Cerridwyn, she sits with her cauldron beneath the earth protecting the cycle of life, death, and rebirth. She has made a deal with her Granddaughter, Kern the maiden of youth (who rests with her Grandmother beneath the earth during this time period) that she can return to the surface in the spring with Rhiannon she must return each cycle to visit her Grandmother. The north is what crowns you. It is the place from where you must begin and to where you must return.

The East represents the energy of Kern returning on the wings of Brigit's Geese graced in the land of Dane. It is the land of Tuatha de Danaan, the people of Danu. It is the time for the new life coming into the great web. In the realm of that which is newly begun, and is rising to the surface. In the east you find a place to set forth your new goals and ideas from, making good use of the rising light and golden sun to find warmth and joyfulness.

The South, is the realm of Arta, the Goddess round and full and heavy laden with the promise of fulfilling the new cycle. It is that energy which is the foundation of one's questions and the bringing of things to their fullest point. This is the time when you must bring that which you set about to its fullest point as this will indicates the most you can attain in any situation.

The West is the realm of the goddess Banba, one of the triple Goddess. She represents the lamenting of the Mother Earth for the dying Sun. In this land the sun sets and that which has grown and born fruit begins to die away. It is that which is leaving the cycle of the questioner's path. For the questioner it is the time to take stock and have a look at what you have accomplished in the cycle past.

The bottom of the cup represents the inner challenges that are part of the questioner's deep self. The bottom of the cup tells you that you must look deep in yourself and understand the self for the meaning to be made manif-est.

If you have a lot of symbols appearing at the bottom of your cup you may want to keep a piece of Ivy near you for a while. Ivy will help you to focus the intensity of the work that you need to do. The bottom most part of the cup represents the furthest away in terms of when something will occur because you have to understand something of yourself before it can come to pass.

The top of the cup represents the here and now. The top of the cup is the beginning and what is at hand so you must be alert and observe fully what is going on around you. Let the universe guide you and listen with both your inner and outer ears.

The web of life is what the culmination of the energies in your cup represents. It is what your cycle in the next year will draw to you.

Nota Bene: Remember that these matters are only shadows and once you have seen them you can learn from them and maximise you efforts in planning your life.

Reading the Cup

If, once the cup is lifted, the tea drops quickly, there is a sorrow approaching and the questioner will be disappointed in their anticipation. DO not be alarmed, as the Wise folk believe that forewarned is forearmed. Additionally, this does not mean that all is lost and something better may be in store for you. If the tea drops slowly, it means a time of relative happiness or content-ment.

Look at the bottom of the cup and if there is no sugar present or just a little then no great luck will befall the questioner in this cycle. If there is a lot of sugar left then they will be very lucky.

Observe around the rim of the cup and if there are any particles then this is good news by post. This can also be interpreted to mean that the questioner shall hear from someone they will find happiness in hearing from.

Turn the cup slowly in a clockwise fashion. Look for

letters first which would form initials. The presence of these would indicate the person(s) that will be involved with the questioner's progress of answer. Then look for numbers or roman numerals. This often will indicate the time frame.

Usually time is lots of three, three hours, days, weeks or months. The closer to the bottom of the cup the longer the time frame.

It is important to pay attention to this part of the reading first as it sets the stage for what the other symbols will mean when they come together.

The reader must always start from the season that is at hand first and proceed around the cup. This will correctly line up the sequence of events.

There are two rules to consider and follow.

> 1. If a symbol appears on its own, then it is a foretelling, sometimes symbols will be grouped together and one has to piece together their meaning. Add this meaning to the time frame and any numbers or initials that may be present around it and there you have an answer of foretelling.

> 2. Another rule that the old religion is very strict about is casting. What this means is that if you see something very negative in a cup you phrase the information in such a way as not to cast it. This means you do not project out into the world. Let me give you an example.

About Casting - Denise

I read the teacup of a very dear friend once and she was asking about her relationship with her father. They had not spoken for over four years and she had heard that he was retiring. As this was a big step for him, she was very distressed. Her question was as to how to make it possible to arrange a reconciliation with him and whether it was going to be possible.

When I looked inside her cup, I saw that in association with her father there was a bridge in the north of her cup, quite close to the top. This was next to a bird. This formed the picture that her father would soon be taking flight across the bridge between the two worlds. I was forbidden to say anything like, "oh, your father is going to die very soon," as that is casting. What I was allowed to say is "that there appears to be a crossing and that I advise you, very strongly, to just go and see him and spend as much time with him as you can over the next few weeks and mend any rifts between you". I told her to take some photos of when she was little with him in them. She did as I advised and had a wonderful two weeks. When he went through (suffered) an aneurysm and was lying near death in the hospital she was so grateful that I had told her in the way that I had done. He died after they had shared love and having made peace between them. If I had cast for her, the vision of his passing, I would have been sending him that negative energy and would have been the focus of the time they had together. This would have cast a cloud of gloom and unhappiness instead of enabling them to enjoy each other's company is a positive way.

ents of Style"

d reader is able to find positive ways of nting not so happy news. Life has its good side and its bad patches, but have the warning we can prepare for that which is to come, as make better use of time.

Taking Notes

You can always ask that your reading be taped but it is better not to have electrical equipment in use while you are in session. I always recommend finding some very special notepaper. Then you can note points of interest or importance. There are some shops that still sell handmade paper. That is by far the best for the purpose.

If you can't find it don't worry, even a paper bag or a used envelope will do. If the exercises at the beginning of a reading are done correctly, you will remember most of what is revealed anyway as it is a part of you and it is simply being brought into conscious mind.

Remember that there is now a connection between the inner and outer selves on these levels so recalling what you are told is as simple as recalling the properties of an apple.

Wishes

Learning the art of tea leaf reading, like anything else worthwhile in life takes time and patience. It will require thought and study. Do not be afraid to refer to the symbol index when you are unsure.

I wish you blessings upon your journey and hope that the lessons imparted in this book will open you to a future of higher understanding and peace within yourself and with the world around you.

Blessed Be   [bendith arnom]

INDEX

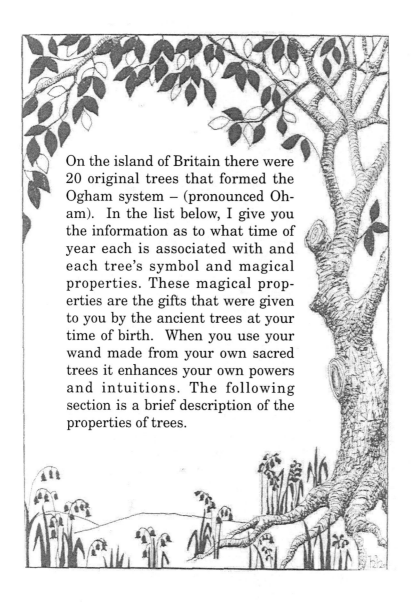

On the island of Britain there were 20 original trees that formed the Ogham system – (pronounced Oh-am). In the list below, I give you the information as to what time of year each is associated with and each tree's symbol and magical properties. These magical properties are the gifts that were given to you by the ancient trees at your time of birth. When you use your wand made from your own sacred trees it enhances your own powers and intuitions. The following section is a brief description of the properties of trees.

The Ogham Alphabet

A/Birch
23rd December to 20th January:
The Birch tree offers you new starts and beginnings. It represents birth, rebirth, fertility, new ideas, opportunities, a journey, an initiation, a cleanser, a nourishment. It is the time of passage and a connection to youth-fulness, leaving behind the old patterns.

B/Rowan (or Mountain Ash)
21st January to 17th February:
The Rowan offers you protection from harmful influences. It represents your intuition and insights, increased psychic powers, energies for divinations spiritual strength, and growth. Additionally it offers you tenacity in hard times.

C/Ash
18th February to the 17th March:
The Ash tree offers you a key to universal truth, every action in the universe has a reaction, interlocking circles of life, death, and rebirth. The Ash represents the power to manifest positive affirmations.

D/Gorse
21st March Vernal Equinox: The Gorse offers you a gathering in, a synthesis with underlying energy. It represents the coming together of inner and outer forces.

E/Alder
18th March to 14th April:
Alder offers you the elements of fire and water. Alder represents the active and receptive part of your intuitive self, balance, preservation, protection in challenges. It is the tree of a spiritual warrior, confidence to go forward where the path darkens.

F/Willow
15th April to 12th May:
The willow offers insight into the unconscious expression of emotions. It represents to you, your intuitions, the moon, dreams that manifest best under the cloak of darkness, the ability of psychic perceptions.

G/Hawthorn
13th May to 9th of June:
Hawthorn offers you the ability to understand universal love, the true aspects of human benevolence. It represents the heart and cleansing of blocked energy being released and the spirit being prepared for new growth.

H/Heather
21st June – Summer Solstice:
Heather offers you the opening of a gateway between the material and the spiritual world. It represents focus on the fiery passion of healing, a lifting of one's spirits and the outgoing caring for others in need.

I/Oak
10th of June to 7th July:
The great Oak offers you, your inner strength, forti-
tude, courage and self-determination. It represents a
doorway to your inner strength and longevity.

j/Holly
8th July to 4th August:
The Holly offers you restored balance and energy. It
represents directions restored and communications
open. Additionally Holly offers you the place where
unconditional love abides in the heart. For you, life's
responsibility continually takes on new love and
happiness.

k/Hazel
5th August to 1st September:
The sacred Hazel tree offers you divine visions of the
future. It represents depth of your listening intuitions,
as with such skill the essence of knowledge is revealed
to you. You grow and become a being of deep wisdom,
transformation, a catalyst for facilitating the flowing of
life for itself.

l/Apple
Universal:
The Apple tree is a Witches most Sacred of all Trees.
The Goddess hides in her star in the centre of the
apple's fruit. The Apple offers you the magical forces of
the Goddess energy. It enables an abundant and open

heart through the triple aspect of life.

m/Aspen or White Poplar
22nd September Autumnal Equinox:
The Aspen or White Poplar offers you the gift of listening to the inner self. This represents the support of unconditional love, truth and trust; great links to the eternal source.

n/Vine
2nd September to the 29th September:
The Vine offers you the uniting with other, and the skill of teaching the universal truths. It represents determination and instincts through the loosening of inhibitions.

o/Ivy
30th September to 27th October:
Ivy demands the restricting search for the self. From this search and understanding of the self, Ivy offers you greater depth of attachments, freedoms of decision, and union.

q/Broom or Reed
28th October to 24th November:
The broom offers you cleansing of spirit and the ability to bring cleansing about in others and in the land around you. It represents the restoration of harmony and the utilization of Astral Travel.

R/Elder

24th November to the22nd December:
The Elder gives you transformation and renewal.
Through constant efforts of transformation, you find
regeneration and refinement of the wisdom of an elder.

S/Blackthorn

Universal:
The Blackthorn represents a challenge which is an
enforcement of fate. Blackthorn represents the ability
to traverse difficult situations, choosing your perspect-
ive positive outcome.

T/Fir

Universal:
The great fir tree represents objectivity and far seeing
inner wisdom. If gives the gift of ever life, cycling in
every season keeping the promise of life eternal alive.

U/Yew

Universal:
The Yew tree represents the cycle of death and rebirth,
never ending cycle transformation. The Yew offers you
access to the ancestors and spiritual realms that
contain the secrets which make up what life is, that
exists today and tomorrow.

Once you have decided on what wood you will use and
gathered your piece, whittle down each end to a blunt
point and rub it down with bee's wax to smoothen. You

can peal the bark off the rest of the wood and decorate it as you would like or simply leave it plain.

Symbols in the Tea Leaves

Here is a directory of the various symbols that may appear in your cup. You will notice that most of the symbols are not related to modern technological inventions but relate to the earth and natural elements. This is due to what is in your own natural energy. If modern symbols do appear then use them as representing the immediate "outer energy", around you and how it connects with your inner self. The symbols are listed in alphabetical order.

Acorn: Since the acorn is the seed of an oak tree it represents increase in something that has or will have enormous strength or great stature. It is prosperity and bounty. If found in the north, the increase is on its way. In the east, it is about to grow. In the south it is coming to its fullness and in the west you are harvesting your bounty.

Anchor: The anchor is usually the symbol of something being in one place for a time - unmoving, waiting for the right moment to proceed. In the north, this means that there will be no movement or progress for a while. In the east, it means that there will be some growth but that it will be held back. In the south it means that coming into its fullness will be slowed down and in the west it means a delayed harvest of bringing one's fortune to one's self.

Angel: While this symbol only emerged with the import of Christianity on the British Isles or Isles of the Mighty and the Blessed, the wise folk always associate angels and fairies together. This symbol represents the light and magical side of ones being. In the north, it means that a wondrous event is about to enter the cycle of ones life. In the east, it means that the magic of life is starting to grow for you. In the south, it means that the fairy folk are protecting your affairs and will see that there is great magic in all that you do. In the west, the fairies guide the wisdom that you gather to insure that you do not forget that life at any stage has its own magic.

Ant: This symbol wherever it appears in your cup usually means achievements. Where it appears usually signifies what season it will take place in.

Anvil: the symbol represents the work and labour of your hands. It is honest toil. It is the means toward accomplishment.

Apple: The apple is the symbol of the star of the wise. If you cut an apple around rather than through its stem, you can see the witch's star where the fairy of rebirth hides. If you get this symbol in your cup, it is very lucky indeed. If you have it in the north it represents the coming of many new and magical things of change and plenty. In the east, it means that which

may be hidden from immediate sight is about to make itself seen. In the south, the apple is the full fruit, that which carries promise off fulfilment in whatever you do. In the west it is a sure sign that whatever you have begun will come to its right conclusion for you.

Arm: The arm in any part of the cup tell one that guidance or council should be sought on the matter of the question, it symbolises the reaching out.

Arrow: The arrow is for direction, for movement, and to have an arrow in any quarter is a sign that all is moving as it should. If the arrowhead is pointed in a counter clockwise direction, it means to take a step back and reassess.

Axe: The axe means division, it represents a path which branches into two directions and you are feeling ambivalent about it. In the east, the axe represents two new ideas one will eventually become stronger. In the south, it represents two offers, in the west, it represents two departures and in the north, it represents two options.

Baby: A baby actually represents youthfulness, or an idea in its infancy. Only when the symbol is found in the north does it represent an actual new arrival or the heralding of a pregnancy. In the east, it represents the birth of something longed for. In the south, it represents that which is longed for being delayed in coming to fruition in the west it represents something not coming to its full development or potential.

Barn: Or storage building represents abundance. This is not monetary wealth but in terms of stock or material items. In the north, it represents the coming of material gain, in the east the beginnings or the pathway opening for material progress, in the south a barn represents, fulfilment of the abundance and in the west you have reached your maximum levels.

Barrel: This represents an emptiness that needs filling. In the north, it is the time when you can plan and dream how to fill this void in your life. In the east, the barrel represents something coming in and there is the potential of the need being filled. If in the south it represents that the void will definitely be filled with contentment.

Basket: Baskets represent gathering. In the north, the basket presents an adventure, the deciding on

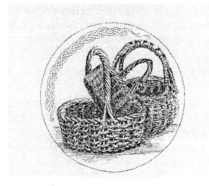

what will be sought after. In the east, the beginning of the journey being open to knowledge and signposts will be of great advantage. In the south, the basket represents the taking in of gifts from the universe and in the west the basket means that you can now look with introspection at the wonderful things you have gained in the past year and give thanks.

Bat: The bat is a warning of treachery. In the north it represents someone plotting against you or contriving to do you harm. In the east someone is setting into motion, a negative action aimed at you. In the south it represents harm is about to befall you and gives you the opportunity to do a protection spell or carry a protection talisman. While this is a negative symbol, it has a good purpose in that you can be made aware and take measure to protect yourself for harm and neutralize anything coming toward you.

Bear: This is a powerful symbol, one of the totems of the Moon. The bear is represented as the pregnant Goddess the power of life and rebirth. In the North therefore, the bear is the symbol of that which is about to enter in the new cycle and awaits rebirth. In the east, the bear represents the new life or idea growing but remains unborn. In the south the bear represents the time just before birth before someone or thing is set forth into the world. In the west, the new life has been born and is cast into life.

Bed: Bed is a caution symbol usually means that you are pushing too hard. This is a general symbol and no matter where it occurs in the wheel of your cup and life you should take it to mean that in that particular season where it falls, you must take extra rest and not push either yourself or that which is attempted or you will not prevail.

Beetle: The beetle is a good little creature to have anywhere in your cup. It signifies luck and happiness and if it is near a negative symbol, it will cancel it out. Additionally, if it falls after a negative symbol it means an end to that negativity.

Bell: The bell is announcing something, news on its way. In each season, the bell can herald something coming. It depends on what it is near as to the nature of the news. Look for the nearest symbol and that will tell you the nature of the news.

Bird: The bird means that you will soon be hearing news of a journey. This is a journey to another place. The location of the bird in the cup will tell you when the right time to make that journey would be. As the universe has a grand program for everything in its own time, it would be wise to head the time frame that the cup will reveal.

Boat: Travel by water, again, pay attention to when in your cup this symbol lands. Travel by water can be dangerous at certain times of the year depending on where it is you are destined to go. Look around the Boat for other symbols, which might lead to where the trip will take you if you do not have one planned at the moment.

Bone: While in some cases such as a skull and cross-bones the bone can mean danger of death, a bone by itself means permanence. As the body dies away, bones remain for hundreds and even thousands of years. If a bone appears in the north it means that survival will be assured through the coming cycle and that, you will live a long and prosperous life. In the east, it means that ideas and projects born in this time will enjoy prosperity and will succeed. If the bone is found in the south, there will be no problem with putting your ideas or projects out into the world and that they will last. In the west, the bone binds the fluidity of ideas with other things in your life.

Book: A book has two meanings, if the book is an open book then secrets and learning will come to you. If the book is closed the information that you seek will not be revealed to you at this time. Usually you find another symbol later on that will indicate the revealing of the answers you seek in another location in your cup. This tells you that while it is not time yet for you to know that answer there will be some indic-ation as to when the answer will come to you.

Bottle: A bottle represents wisdom contained. If the bottle is uncorked, in the north the bottle represents the wisdom that is about to be given to you. In the east, you are beginning to open to the knowledge you seek, in the south you are filled with the wisdom that you need to carry on and take charge of your life, look within and in the west a bottle tells you that you can pour the wisdom backward and give it to those who need it. If the bottle is corked, in any area of the cup it means that you are blocked and need to lay back and be peaceful for a time and that which you seek will be revealed.

Bow: The bow represents the hunt. It does not mean actually hunting down of other creatures. It means that you are going to look for something that is not readily obvious. It is time to go and seek new adventures and ideas. In the north, it is awareness that all is not fulfilled, in the east it is the organizing of your directions in the south it is active seeking and in the west it is making that which has not been obvious to manifest.

Box: The box tells of a gift, some thing that you do not expect. It may not be in the form of a gift like a birthday present, but something that comes to you for no real reason at all and is a joy and blessing in your life.

Bridge: Bridges foretell change. They represent transition in your life. This can seem confusing and difficult as it often means a change of circumstances including a change of location. It can also represent leaving the old behind but remaining connected to it. In the north, it means that in the new cycle, you will be making some drastic changes and it is a good time to plan and prepare. In the east it means the bridge to new and bright horizons, in the south the bridge is finally achieving your goal and in the west, it is a crossing over, now that the work is done, to a time of rest and passivity. If someone is very old and very ill, it can mean that it is the passing between the two worlds, of death in this world into the time before beginning to await rebirth.

Broom: The broom represents a clean sweep. It means a casting off of old baggage clearing out useless or dead relationships and making the way for new. In the north, the broom represents a preparing of the way. In the east the broom represents the dawn of the day and the vision of what may be to come. In the south, the broom represents a cleared path and a coming in of the new. In the west, it represents the clearing out for a time of rest before beginning again.

Bull: The bull is the symbol of force. If it falls in the season of your birth within your cup it means that your inner power will come to your aid and give you abounding strength and resolution to make things happen. In the north, it represents the force of determination. In the east, it represents strength in the making that is now about to take hold. In the south it is the strength to push something through to its fullest and in the west the force to see something through to its conclusion.

Butterfly: Shape shifting. This represents the ability to change, to let that which is inside of you out, to transform. If a change in your life is needed this is the correct symbol. If in the north, it is the time to plan what the best changes are for your own person and why they are needed. In the east, the sun warms the inner part of your being and you can see the path ahead for change, in the south the changes are coming to pass and in the west the changes are completed and you can move ahead in the next cycle.

Candle: Candles are always the symbol of illumination. They represent the lighting of the path, so whatever location in your cup they

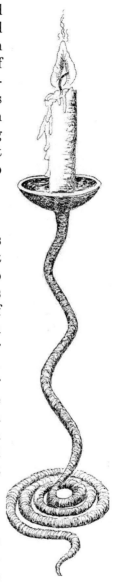

land it is always a very positive and uplifting symbol.

Cane: A cane is the symbol of needing to take the council of another. In the north it represents the asking for inspiration, in the east it means that you should collab-orate with someone for new directions. In the south a cane means that in this endeavour you will need a co-partner that you can rely on and in the west it means that you can no longer go it alone. In other words, you should realise that accepting assistance can make a positive difference that you have been resisting.

Castle: The building of dreams. A castle means the building of new and exciting prospects, only on a grand scale. It is looking at the whole picture and deciding to make a go of it. In the north, it is the castle that is hidden or unspoken dream, in the east it is the setting into motion the realisation of that dream. In the South, a castle means fulfilling that dream and your life is at its zenith. In the west, you have your dream, you are where you should be in life. Count your blessings as riches.

Cat: Cats are the symbol of luck. They are the profound source of psychic revelation in your life. If you have a cat in your cup you are lucky and if the cat is looking out for your best interest both on the physical and the psychic plane. The cat guards you and brings you luck in every quarter.

Cauldron: The cauldron is the wisewoman's symbol of the cycle of life, death and rebirth. In the North the goddess Cerridwyn, the grandmother of time sits with the cauldron and promises us that all that sits within the earth or the cosmos will find rebirth but must return to her at the end of the cycle for a time of rest. In the east, the cauldron is the awaking, the spirit rising to new heights. In the south, the cauldron is life, holding the wisdom and the joy for life of all that is past, all that is, and all that will be. In the west the cauldron heralds the season of the time for the lying down.

Chair: The chair, like the bed, is the symbol of the need to rest, to take some time out and reflect on things that are around you for the moment. This is relevant in any location in your wheel.

Circle of dots: A circle of dots is incompletion. In the north it means that there is little chance of completion to any full meaning. If it is in the east it means that unless you pay attention to the groundwork you are laying down now the plan will be incomplete and will not thrive. In the south, it is the diminished returns due to bad planning and in the west, disappointment and lack of accomplishment, a lesson to be learned about paying attention when making plans.

Claw: A claw is a warning of physical danger usually work related of some nature. Take head and beware accordingly. The claw is telling you to be observant and not to be careless or you may get hurt.

Clouds: This is another symbol that means the same where ever it falls. Clouds represent passing gloom. If this has been a particularly bad or gloomy patch for you then it is telling you that they are passing. They also may herald a period of stagnation. Use this time well and know that all times get overfed with and this too shall pass. You will be better for time out.

Clover: This means a sudden boost of good fortune right when you need it most. It can mean in the east a lucky break when starting something. In the south, clover is indicative of exceptional abundance and productivity. In the west it can mean that you suddenly actualise most that you thought you had and be very happy and content.

Cobweb: the means that you are, or are to be shielded by someone. In the north, it means being protected from harsh conditions; in the east protected from bad decisions; in the south protected from greed, and; in the west protected from melancholy. It can be the protecting of one from one's negative self.

Coffin: This is not the symbol of physical death. It is the laying to rest and putting behind you of old matters. It is a leaving behind, a cut free. In all quarters, it means a release from that which has been obstructing you.

Comb: The comb is for untangling and making straight. In the north, it sets things into a focused order. In the east, it brings in the new in a logical and organized way. In the south, the abundance will be straightforward and uncomplicated and in the west, the rest period will be orderly and unencumbered.

Cow: The cow is another totem animal. It is the symbol of easy birth. This in the north means re-emergence, such as starting back to work after a period of absence. In the east the appearance of a cow represents the entering of a new sphere such as a change in job titles. In the south, it is giving new life to one's self and one's circumstances. In the west, the cow is safe conduct.

Crab: The crab represents the ability to observe small details. In the north, it reminds you that in making plans to look at the small print. In the east, the crab tells you to go slowly and make plans with the smallest of detail. The crab in the south tells you to slow down you are moving ahead to fast and observe that which is around you before you move ahead. In the west, the crab is the watery creature that lives with the ebb and flow. This position tells you to go more with the flow and stop fighting so hard.

Cradle: The cradle is the cycle fulfilled. It also can indeed herald the coming of a new baby. It is best if the cradle appears in the south or the east depending on other matters in your life.

Crown: The crown is the circle of wisdom ever growing. In the north, it means that you are about to increase your inner wisdom. This wisdom comes to you in the east, is put to full use in the south and in the west you pass it along as the elder.

Cup: This symbol represents to you the drinking from the cup of life. This tells you to be more connected with the life force and the ebb and flow of the seasons. It tells you for you to appre-ciate all that comes to you for even the smallest things, is given in grace and offered as a blessing from the mother earth.

Diamond shape:
This symbol means
you will be given a
representative gift
of adornment.
This is usually
jewellery to mark
the occasion such
as a term of
endearment, like
love, or the symbol
or everlasting love
such as a wedding
ring.

Dish: The dish means that you
will never want. This does not necessarily mean in
terms of money. It means that you will always feel
that your life has meaning and that if you look
carefully where ever this falls in your teacup that you
always have what you need and sometimes more.

Dog: A dog is a true and loyal friend,
not just an acquaintance but also a
long-term friend. If this is in the
North it can mean that you have
someone watching over you or that,
you are about to meet that person.

In the east, it is the meeting of a new friend, and in the south, it is that friendship enjoying the fullness of it. The friend in the west represents a friend in times of need of strife, someone who is there to comfort and guide you.

Door: A door indicates that you may not be aware of that which may lie ahead. If in the north, the door is a portal, a place where all things begin. In the east, a door is a good thing being opened up to you. A door in the south means something that you must realise before the fullness of that which you seek can appear and in the west, it is the time before crossing over.

Dragon: The dragon is the guardian of the well of knowledge. If you want to drink from the well, you must prove yourself worthy by purifying yourself and walking a straight and worthy path.

Egg: The egg is the symbol of rebirth. If the egg is found in the north, it is the symbol that an entity is ready for rebirth. If it appears in the east the egg means that the promise of rebirth is progressing. If in the south rebirth is imminent. If the egg is found in the west, then it is the symbol of something about to die away and enter the womb of rebirth. This is usually a positive symbol in that one can be reassured that all is progressing as it should.

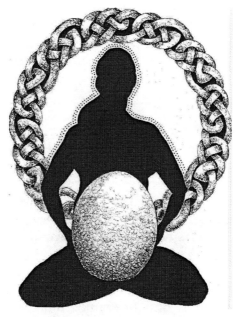

Eye: The eye represents one's ability to see the inner self. The third eye is a symbol recognised throughout many cultures. It tells us that we can see not only on this plane but the psychic plane as well. The third eye draws in energy from other levels and helps us to assess that which is around us. In the north, the third eye directly correlates with energies that are not in a physical form and tells us that someone is around us. In the east, the third eye tells us to examine other levels of consciousness to find the place of new beginnings. In the south, the third eye tells us how to recognise spiritual fulfilment and in the west, it tells us how to prepare what we know for better use.

Face: This represents the self. Where ever the face is found in the cup look at the nearest symbols to find out what it is in conjunction with.

Fan: This symbol is the reminder that pride goes before a fall and that false pride can lead to downfall.

Feather: The feather represents the winged creatures and the ability to soar above it all. If this symbol appears in the north it tells you to look beyond the material world to the spiritual side of yourself. If it is in the east it tells you that the breath of the winds will carry you above the current crisis. In the south, it tells you that not only will it carry you above your crisis but also it will help you to see a resolution. In the west, the feather has carried you to safety and the world is restored to balance for you.

Finger: Forewarns you of a problem ahead and to be on the look out. It is usually close to the symbol, which will tell you the nature of the problem.

Fire: Fire represents the passions. In the old religion the cross quarters are all fire holidays. This is because they represent the passions of life for its self. The most ideal place to find this symbol is half way between the northern, eastern, southern and western points. In the north, fire represents the stated position, waiting for the correct moment for movement. In the east, it represents the passions of all that is coming in, love and laughter, light and happiness. In the south, it represents the serious passions, the deep and abiding love, the willingness to pass through love's flame for that which will endure. In the west, it represents that which cannot be extinguished by time. The fire of passion, of life's love and longing for it crosses time and space and knows no bounds and limits. It is important to remember this in life.

Fireplace: The fireplace is the heart of the household, around the hearth beats the unity of the family. If a fireplace appears in your cup in the North, East or south it represents a binding together of family, of solidity in the relationships. If this symbol appears in the west, it is a warning of disharm-ony and the reminder that home and hearth are the central priority in one's life.

Fence: Fences are hurdles that we have to overcome, these are usually meant to make us take a look at something before we leap. A fence in the North is representative of time not yet at hand and that another cycle must pass. In the east, a fence represents a delayed arrival. In the south, it cautions us not to be too hasty and to make sure all the details are seen to. In the west, we must not rush into getting it all done and finished too quickly.

Fish: Fishes represent the fluid self, our ability to change direction and be flexible. It represents psychic ability and intuition. In each quarter, it admonishes us to look into the depths and to ask ourselves the deeper questions in life, not to just live on the surface.

Flower: Flowers are taken as compliments, kind remarks that, at the time, do not seem significant, but have a ripple effect which in turn has a profound effect. A kind word can change one's mood and effect how one reacts to a situation. This in turn can change a whole sequence of events no matter where in the cup it falls it is a very positive symbol.

Foot: A journey, in life we are on a journey, a journey for the refinement of the spirit or ethos. A foot or feet in a tea cup shows that you are on such a journey and is an indicator. In the north, it tells you that you are awaiting the commencement of a new journey sure to come. In the east, you are heading for the horizon, ever illusive but none the less constant. The quest forever continuing new horizons. In the south, it means that your journey will be full of enrichment and in the west that your journey will give you great prosperity.

Fork: Means group efforts to abundance. The old religion teaches that many hands make light work and through group effort, much can be accomplished. A fork can indicate that by using each other's unique energy toward the whole, the whole will benefit greatly. It is a symbol of movement toward the unity of a better or greater community.

Fox: The fox indicates cunning and warns you to use cunning in making choices. In the north, cunning can indicate a stormy patch in a relationship. In the east it can bring about the truth into light, in the south the cunning of the fox ensnares deceit, and in the west cunning is the undoing of the deceiver.

Frog: You do not like change if the frog appears in your teacup. It represents stubborn will and can be one's undoing unless one is willing to move and change. Making sudden and unwise leaps can be harmful. This symbol most often represents the need to change either jobs or house and the reluctance to do so. In the north, it represents unwillingness to accept the ideas. In the east, it represents procrastination. In the south, it can mean leaping into fruition too late, and in the west missing the boat completely.

Goat: The goat represents the strength of will and of character in times of difficulty. In the north, it is the tenacity to stick by one's goals and ideals even when there are great obstacles. In the east, it is the energy to get going when the going is difficult. In the south, it is the seeing through of a project against all odds and in the west, it is gaining great success despite all.

Grapes, bunch of: Family matters. If a bunch of grapes appears to the north, it is the indicator of an increase in the family. In the east is represents that the family will change locations, such as a house move. In the South, a bunch of grapes tells us that family unity will come to pass and that any family strife will be resolved and the love and harmony of each member will find its place within the whole. In the west, it is solidity, each family member, while eventually going her or his own way, will always remain close to the central family base.

Hammer: The hammer has had many interpretations. Here there are two, depending what symbols are in the areas immediately around it. The first is that the hammer is judgment. If the hammer is down it means that judgment is at hand and will be blind. If the hammer is presented upright then the decision is not yet made and prudent actions will be recommended. The second meaning is that the hammer represents hard work, and the binding together. In the north it means through hard work, the dream that is being dreamed will have a chance. In the east, the dream is awakening and the work starting. In the south, the fire for completion, for accomplishment is the compelling force and the work toward the dream had brought the dream to its reality. In the west, the hammer signifies completion and the time to enjoy the fruits of one's toil.

Hand: A hand in your cup tells you that someone is in need of your assistance. This assistance is in the form of advice or actual physical care. Look for initials around the hand and where it falls in your cup. This is a symbol also to alert you to the needs of others. Do a careful self-check to see if you may be a little selfish about some-thing, or are taking too much in a relationship rather than given enough back. Each of the seasons has its own need to reach out to others and the more you can do it without self-interest the more benevolent the deed. This is a good character-building symbol.

Hat: The hat represents secrets yet to be told. In the North it is that which lies but beyond the conscious spirit. In the east, it is that which is about to make its presence known. In the south, the hat is 'things' going on behind your back, and in the west, the hat is

deception that has been successful. This is a warning symbol. It tells you to look more deeply and to pay attention to that which is going on around you. Having the symbol appear in your cup tells you that it might be a good time to meditate and understand the subtle hints that you are tending to overlook. This will arrest the deception.

Haystack: The symbol reminds us that we reap what we sew. If we sew the seed of good and happiness in life, then happiness and goodness   will come upon us. If we sew other things in life, then those are the things that will come upon us. In the old religion, we believe that what we sow comes upon us three fold, from above, from below as well as from the time at hand. In the north, a haystack tells us to prepare well and think hard upon what we are about. In the east the haystack tells us that what is rising has good potential if well intended. In the south, this symbol represents a good return for what we have put out. The haystack in the west represents what we have sown and what it has reaped.

Headstone: A headstone in your cup represents the death of someone, which has greatly affected your life. This is a death that has caused a great turning point. It is a marker, a representation of the distinction between both worlds. This energy has arrived in your cup to remind you that everything here exists in the spirit form. It only exists in the physical form for a short time. If you despair too long for the physical form you will loose the precious time you have here on that which has gone before and not gain the fullness of your experience here. This tells you that it is time to do a meditation and draw to you that person or animal whose death has caused you such disturbance. Ask that spirit energy for peace and guidance. This symbol when appearing in the North, tells you that someone who has passed maybe about the re-enter, you may soon hear of a pregnancy. If it appears in the east it is the knowledge being given to you, that rebirth can give new life to that which seemed lost. In the south, it is a marker that you must take unto yourself a new attitude to be able to fulfil your destiny. In the west, the marker is the symbol of the passage of the old and the waiting period now come to rest and gather your thoughts.

Heart shape: Unlike most traditional understandings that the heart represents love, it in fact, represents sexual attraction. This is the symbol of lust and the heated fire and passion of life wanting to reproduce its self - the blending of energies. In the north, the passions sleep and are waiting for the new cycle. In the east, the passions are gathering and growing and enjoying the light of the new sun. In the south, the passions have found their goal and are bringing new life forward. This could be considered both in terms of an emotional relationship but also in terms of a new baby. In the west the heart represents the sexual bond has been completed and you need look no more.
Be happy where you are.

Hills: Some thing to overcome before you can see your way ahead. Wherever this appears in your cup it is time to stand back and make sure you have dealt with all aspects of any situation clearly, and be sure of your plan. This is an action symbol and tells you that you must move ahead, get a clear and definite picture of what lies ahead.

Hoe: The hoe is telling you of a desire that you have not paid attention to achieve in some area. You must look to undiscovered talents and longing. In the north, the symbol asks you to look within and find that inner talent, skill that you have left undeveloped. In this day and age, many of the old skills and talents of human beings have gone by the wayside, those which took time and patience and made us slow down and pay attention to one thing at a time. In the east, this symbol tells you that the sun will help you to see some of the hidden aspects. In the south, you have the opportunity in front of you to develop and enjoy your skills. In the west, it tells you that you will succeed having uncovered new and exciting aspects of yourself and will prosper as a result.

Hook: The hook represents a time of inquiry. This is the symbol that represents the desire to capture that which is not known and be able to draw knowledge to one's self. In the north, it is the unknown that begins the adventure. In the east, it is the quest and the question raised. In the south it is the source of knowledge found and in the west, it is the knowledge drawn in from around you and it is to be enjoyed.

Horn: The horn is the symbol of moving forward toward self-awareness and appreciation. Often in life, we search for what we need to know about ourselves from without and we actually need to look within. In the north, the horn heralds a new cycle of growth. In the east, the horn awakens our spirit with the rising sun. In the south, the horn sounds the charge forward into the unknown of self, bringing it fully to light for us to see and enjoy. The west the horn represents the time of coming to a full and right understanding of all that we are.

Horse: The horse symbolises two things. It is, therefore, one of the few symbols in the cup that can have two meanings and is determined by what is in the nearest proximity to the horse. Its lesser meaning is travel by land. A running horse symbolizes a speedy journey overland if it is accompanied by a landmass.

The second meaning is an urgent message on its way. You can tell which one it is as the horse with a message is located quite close to the rim of the cup. With travel news, there are no particular seasonal aspects.

With messages, if they appear at any other level in the cup than the rim area then they have different type of message meaning. In the north a running horse means there is imminent change coming and you should prepare. In the east, it means that life will suddenly charge ahead and you would be wise to go with it. In the south the running horse is time running out and you need to bring your project to its fullest point as soon as you are able. In the west a running horse is that time on this planet is at its ebb. A horse that is standing still tells you to be observant, that your inner

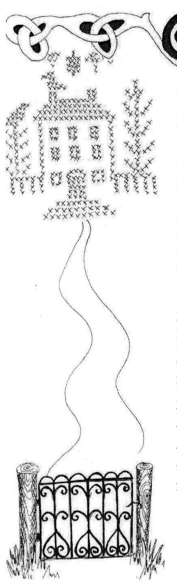

House: This symbol represents home and hearth. A house tells you that you are likely to change homes and if it is near a horse or other land animal or what used to be called a beast of burden then it will be a move within the distance that beast could carry you.

If there is a bird by the house then your move is likely to be a long distance one. In the north, a house is the change in the offing. In the east, the move will be for a better and new beginning. In the south, it will be due to increase. In the west, it will be to finally settle in one place.

strength and power will be a sure guide.

Horseshoe: A horseshoe brings luck wherever it may fall. Why it is considered lucky is that it is something that protects and as such will protect you from ill fate.

Hurdles: Hurdles are challenges that must be met in order to attain one's goals. In the north, the hurdle is a gate and that gate tells you to be patient that the time will be at hand. In the east, the hurdle tells you to be careful before you rise up too quickly. In the south the hurdle means a lot needs to be done before you can get to a completion point and in the west, it means that there will be a delay in getting your harvest in. In other words, the sailing will not be without challenges.

Jar: A jar means that something needs to be borrowed. In the north, the jar indicates the need to get extra energy as the winter was longer than expected and you did not set up sufficient stores. In real terms it means that you needed longer to plan some-  thing than you thought and your resources may be quite thin. In the east, the jar means that you may need help getting something go- ing. In the south, help finishing off to reach the level of abundance that is attainable. In the west, it is the need for careful planning to fill the larder of life to its fullest and prepare for a still period of careful planning that may take longer than expected. This is a very positive sign, it means that what you are about to attempt will go smoothly and you will have plenty. Wherever this symbol appears in your cup it is a very good omen of harmony and easy flow.

Keg: The keg is a positive symbol. It means the storing up and the having of that which is to be stored. It can mean the accumulation of material goods, of the gathering in of family. Where ever the Keg appears it is a good time to act. In the north, it is the time to make a plan of what is needed. In the east, to set plan into motion, in the south, make it happen, and in the west enjoy the bounty. This is a sign of security and happiness.

Kettle: A kettle is the symbol of hospitality. If this symbol appears in the north , it will be a time to draw in and be cosy around home and hearth. In the east, it is time to make new contacts and invite new friends to gather around your table. In the south, it is the time to gather family and friends, old and new and enjoy each other's company. In the west, gather old friends and revel in the joy that time and memories can bring.

Key: The key represents the unlocking of the hidden self. If a key appears in the north this is a very good omen. It means that you are about to open the door to all your hidden and undiscovered elements that you never dreamed you possessed. In the east, the process begins as you step forward, leaving old and useless habits and ideas about yourself behind. In the south, you bask in the sunshine of all you are and make good use of it. In the west, you look inward, and give thanks for the knowledge that has been passed down and has become part of who you are. The key is the symbol of enlightenment of self. Within the self is the understanding of the universe.

Knife: The symbol is that of division. It can be a parting of the ways of halving something. If it is in the north this means that whatever is anticipated will amount to only half. If in the east, the knife represents the sharing of the workload. In the south, the knife divides and sends in two separate directions so that the whole is divided. In the west, the knife is the lessening of the pain of the separation of partings.

Ladder: The universe has provided you with the means to ascend to your greatest heights. Aim high and climb straight. Keep your eyes on your goal and keep your feet straight. Do not stray your feet or you will loose all that you gain.

Ladle: A ladle tells you that you will discover some news or important information and that you should pass it along. Sometimes news is difficult because your motivation for passing it along could come into question.

In the north this means a careful approach and a well devised plan will insure that what you pass along will be received with the good heart that it is intended. In the east, the air the breath of life will give you the courage of your approach. The south will allow you to put forth all your wisdom and talent to let the message be given with love and trust. In the west, the delivered message has brought about much good.

Lamb: Lambs stand for gentleness. In the north, it tells you to temper your plans with kindness, meekness and gentleness. In the east, it means being sensitive and considerate in all that you attempt. In the south, the lamb is the fullness fulfilment without any force from any direction. In the west, the lamb reminds us that in all things a gentle hand does more good than acting with aggression in our hearts.

Lantern: This represents the pioneering spirit. Those that can forge ahead even if the way is not absolutely clear. This is a symbol of courage. In the north, the lantern alerts one to a journey, a life journey. In the east, that journey is begun only based on faith. In the south, the realisation of the dream and the rewards of faith are at hand. The journey is completed in the west and the contentment for having had the courage and succeeded is ample reward.

Leaf: The leaf alerts you to whispering. It tells you to keep your ears open as someone is prone to talking out of turn. In the east, the gossip spreads like wind over an open field but passes just as quickly. Do not engage or give credibility to it or you will be swept away. In the south, the leaf gives you the power to overcome the gossip and prove, by your own strength and powers the ability to overcome the odds. In the west, the leaf has survived the winds and will slowly one at a time let go and wait for the new life and light to come.

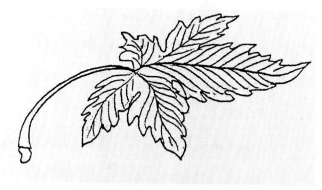

Lightning bolt: In the old world, lightning bolts were considered awesome. They send light across a dark

Letter - alphabet: Letters of the alphabet represent initials of the person involved, look at what symbols are near by and you will be able to tell what they mean. Usually the initials are someone who stands in relationship to the person whose cup is being read.

Letter – mail: This means that an important document is on its way to you. The meaning of this document could have a significant meaning for you if you are wise in your thoughts and actions. Do not react right away to it upon receipt but instead, take time and plan your response well.

sky and illuminated the heavens. When lightning struck the earth it provided a precious source of fire. Fire binds things together. Lightning bolts in a teacup represent in the north a flash of inspiration. In the east they represent the stirring of a passion for something of someone and in the south, the place of fire, lightening ensures that the fires will burn strong and true. In the west, the lightning tells you that even as the sky at night darkens the powers of passion are not lost to the world.

Lizard: Lizards are totem creatures that creep between two worlds. They understand the richness of the dark places on earth. In the north, the Lizard tells you that there is much to be understood in the opposite opinions to what you carry. In the east, it is the living earth breathing life into new ways of looking at the world. In the south, the lizard destroys that which is decayed and in the way of new life. In the west, the lizard finds a comfortable place to dig in for the winter. The west tells you to make yourself comfortable and attend to spiritual business.

Log: The appearance of a log means a gift that brings you love and security. In the north, the log burns in the hearth and provides warmth and light and draws the family to each other. In the east, the log reminds us that the past life is with us and we can draw strength from it. In the south, the log is the foundation upon which we can rely for the fulfilment. In the west, the log symbol is that gift of warmth and comfort which is very precious and we should remember to give as well as to receive.

Mermaid: The mermaid is a creature of magic swimming in the watery depths and knowing the connection between human life and its relationship to the ebb and flow of a fluid nature. In the north, the mermaid is in her depth, she gathers the essences of the bottom of the ocean where the treasures of earth lie, hidden from the sunlight. In the east, the  Mermaid stirs and rises toward the sunlight above, unlike the seed in the Earth, the mermaid can see the glimmering sun the higher she rises. The path becomes more and more illuminated for her. In the south, mermaid reaches the surface carrying her secrets into the light to cast to all those who believe in her existence and what she witnesses. We all need to acknowledge that there are things that may exist even if we cannot see them. In the west, the Mermaid is in her natural element water. She carries to us the old wisdom and we should float with her and beside her to gain the knowledge, she is telling us.

Money: Coinage is increase by trade. It does not necessarily mean monetary riches but instead means that you will have ample to trade. The symbol of coinage tells you that your worries are fruitless and you will not be without. In the north, coins represent richness of spirit that will carry you forward with enough reserves. In the east, coins represent gain, or prosperity that lies ahead through insight. In the south, coins represent a full insight that will be very conducive to growth and expansion. In the west, coins mean that you will have done well at the end of the day and that all that ought to have come to you will.

Moon: Is the Wisewoman's goddess, it is the female deity and the partner of the Sun God. She watches over us in the darkest times. The moon repre-sents the female energy of regen-eration, of the cycle of life, death and rebirth. In the north, the moon is the grand-mother of time that watches, careful that the seeds of the new season are pushed forward to-ward the growing light.

The north actually is the time of midnight when the night sky is at its darkest, also associated with the dark phase of the moon. This is when the promise of time to come is held in the great universal ordering. In the east, the moon is in the youthful growing phase and tells you to enjoy the youthful energy of your feminine side. In the south, the moon is ripe and full and represents the time when the earth hangs heavy-laden with the fruit of the next generation. The south reminds us to bear our heavy burdens in life with joy, the moon watches over us to carry us safely past danger. In the west, the moon represents the time to draw in and the waning moon represents the wisdom of the elder.

Mountain: Where there is a mountain there is a valley and in life just, as we reach our heights we have our depths. In the north, a mountain is when the spirit energy contains all that we need for the next cycle of life and when we start from the valley. A mountain in the east will show us, gain in a steady pace all that we are mean to acquire during this life time. When the mountain appears in the south, it tells us that the summit we are meant to strive for is ahead and that the exertion we are undergoing now will prevail if we keep our eye on the summit. In the west, the mountain is conquered and we see the next valley and beyond that the place where the sun sinks back into the belly of the mother earth for rebirth. In this cycle, we learn that as we climb to the heights we must also climb back down the other side and in the descent take pleasure in having reached the peak.

Mouse: The mouse lays low to the ground and only sees the world in its minute detail. In the north, the mouse tells you to pay attention to the smallest of details in the laying of plans. In the east, it is in watching the ground and noticing the first splits in the ground that one realises that the new life is on its way and should be safeguarded. In the south, the mouse runs through the grown grass that obscures its path with its lush abundance. This tells us not to be blinded by sudden increase and loose our way. In the west, the mouse finds the earth dying away and that she must dig into the safety of the earth like the seed with great care to sleep and dream until the light returns. Like the industrious little mouse, we should be wise as to when the need for wisdom, prudence and rest is required.

Needle: A needle with thread is the finalising of a major decision. It is the weaving together of all your ideas and thoughts on the subject and coming up with the final solution. The unthreaded needle is the heading not to go ahead until all the information is gathered and you have had time to ponder each aspect with due care before binding a plan into action.

Nest: A nest is the making of a home and signifies an engagement. This symbol is of a place that two people can come together to grow together a produce their young. In the north, the nest is the universal plan in its order, be patient as the inevitable will come to pass. In the east, the engagement is announced and the new life cycle for the couple will begin. In the south, the nest will be made and happiness, prosperous and loving family will be the result. In the west, the family home is the centre of well-being and the place to return for comfort. It is the place we should turn when the harsh world bears down on us and we need refuge to regroup and regain our inner strength. It is the place of nurturance and the place from where we should all go forth from.

Numeral: A number usually indicates a time frame although Wise Folk believe that all things happen in three's = three days, weeks or months. Years are usually so difficult to forecast in most cases because many things can alter the sequence of events. The shadows of the future lie in wait but they can be changed or overlooked so they are only taken as probabilities when we take into account our ability to create change. If we pay attention along the way to these shadows, we can avoid many pitfalls.

Oar: Means that you have the controls in your hands and that you are underway. You can temper your journey and take notice of what is around you or you can row quickly to get to your destination. The decision is yours depending upon what is around the oar in your teacup.

Pail: The pail is telling you to bail out of something with haste. You have not made a wise move. In the north, you may be able to catch yourself before you make an unwise decision. In the east, the wind has swept you into unfavourable places, use the wind to blow you clear and into better light. In the south you are bogged down by a wrong turn and you will need to summon your resources to see yourself clear. In the west, you have made a grave error and you will need to ask the help of others to set you back into the correct path.

Pan: The lord of the greenwood and consort to the mother earth. As Lord Pan merrily plays his pipes and the faeries and wood sprites dance, he brings life by impregnating the earth. In the north, Pan plays his pipes and calls life back unto itself. Wait until you feel the right time is at hand before you act. In the east, enjoy the spirit of life and energy around you. In the south, Lord Pan is in his element and rejoices with the mother earth at their bounty. In the west, couples should look toward the strength that their unity brings and make sure that every day they give something back to the Lord and Lady for their gifts.

Pan pipes: The Lord Pan calls to your productiveness. He tells you that you are not being as productive as you could be. This is the wake up call that you may be being a bit lazy on certain fronts that need your urgent attention. Listen to his music and let it lift your spirits and carry you ahead.

Plough: The plough represents mating or the planting of the seed. It is time to prepare the place for the needed seeds. If you are planning a pregnancy, this is the time to ready your body and being for this event. It may be that you need to ready yourself to take on some important work that you will set out upon the world such as writing a book, or producing some music. In the north, the ground is frozen and so you will ready your tools and dream of what you want to have ahead of you. In the east, the time for ploughing and sowing is at hand. Make your planting and offering the seed to the mother earth with all of the gladness of your heart as your efforts will benefit a great many. In the south, the plough is the continued work and labour of your being and your efforts will be blessed and cause increase for all those around you. In the west, the ground is made ready for the next cycle. Finish what you begin and be settled to sit quietly with it for the present.

Pump: This symbol means that you will encounter people who will seek to get as much information from you as possible. In the north, you will be asked secrets of a spiritual nature. In the east, it will be advice to the young, in the south, it will be questions toward your parental instincts and in the west, the questions will draw from your inner wisdom from the elder in you. Remember however, be selective in whom you allow to be in these positions. Cast not your pearls before the swine.

Quill: This is the symbol of getting back to the basics. You have strayed too far into the material world and your distresses are a result. In the north, the quill tells you to sit quietly and look into your inner being. Rediscover your spiritual side. In the east, work with the earth, get the joy from soaking up the energy from the earth, the endowments of that which has lain down and become part of the nourishing for the new life. In the south, remember the earth's bounty, the warm days when the fruit ripens on the trees and the limbs lay heavy from the work of the tree. In the west, remember that you are fruitful like the tree and must produce in order to be replenished.

Rabbit: A rabbit represents a time to be a bit more carefree, to scamper about and simply enjoy the here and now. It is the stopping when you need to nourish yourself and then bounding forward in the sunlight to laugh and play. Whatever season this symbol falls the rabbit tells you not to take yourself too seriously for a while and just to go out and play.

Rainbow: Although you cannot see the colours of the rainbow in your cup you can see a banded arch. The rainbow is a promise and one that tells you that the path to the magical realms to the inner self must be washed clear of all impurities before you can see it. It is then a descent into the perfect light of life that carries the inner ethos. In this ethos is the eternal self. The rainbow is the path to follow to find that self. In the north, the rainbow is the bridge between the time before beginning and the rebirth into the physical world. This means that there may be the coming of a new enlightenment. In the east, the rainbow bridges the life forces - the physical with the ethos. In the south, it means that the ethos is bringing out the inner and ancient knowledge and will couple that with what is being learned here and now. In the west, the rainbow tells us that the bridge to rebirth is through death and we much return to our ethos to yet rise again.

Rake: A rake represents some serious searching for something or someone that is lost. In the north, the rake tells us that we will become aware of something or someone missing. In the east, the search will begin on the right path. The south tells us that the search will prove fruitful and the west is that which has been lost will return.

Rat: Rats mean someone being crafty. It means treachery is around you and you should beware. In the north, the treachery has to do with some ideas that you have given away. Someone may steal them from you. In the east, the rat will undo what you sew by eating the seed before they have chance to take root. In the south, the rat will carry away your abundance before you have a chance to gather it in. The rat in the west is the vermin that feeds on the misfortune of others. If you get a rat in your cup, you can plan how to neutralise it and protect your interests with calling in water, which will drown a rat's ill intent.

Ring: The old wise folk have always believed that a ring is the symbol of eternal energy. In its primary sense, it is life, death and rebirth, but can mean that a particular kind of energy is given forever such as a wedding ring. This pledges that the love with which the ring is given, if properly tended should cycle eternally. In the north, a circle is the promise that the energy will endure cycle to cycle. In the east, the energy will remain young and breath with the breath of new life. In the south, the energy will always produce fulfilment and be bound together in harmony. In the west, the ring is the cycle of completion and that, all things will come around as they are meant to.

Double ring: A double ring is another of the very few symbols that has a double meaning. The correct meaning will be determined by other symbols which are around the symbol in the tea cup. The first meaning is the union of earth and sky, or so above, so below the union of the inner and outer worlds. This can be around you or directly of the self. The second meaning of the double ring signifies a hand fasting or marriage. It is the intertwined life forces of two beings. In the north, the two rings is the symbol of soul mates about to be reunited. In the east, it is two energies being born unto one another, the falling in love and binding of hearts. In the south, the double rings means that the union will take place and in the west, the couple will live a long and happy life together.

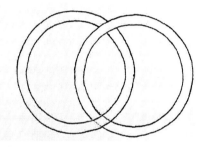

Rope: A rope is the binding together symbolizing the fibres of our lives in a continuous fashion. It is the culmination of life's experience. It is our conscious awareness of all that makes up who we are. In the north, the rope is the beginning of a new phase or chapter in our life. In the east, the rope is a new an innovative energy coming in that will strengthen the fibre of our time here. In the south, the rope is the thickness of the threads the nature of how you are filling your life. Your rope will depend on how hard you work at life. In the west, you will tell by the thickness or thinness how well you are experiencing life. It will tell you that you may need to get out and do more and experience more. It may tell you that you are doing too much and need to be more temperate or it may tell you that you have the balance just right.

Saddle: The saddle tells you that the creatures in your life will look after you and will protect you from your own bad judgements.

Scissors: This is the time of cutting away of that which impedes you. You may not recognise all that impedes you and you will find it hard to bear. In the north, it will be that which is preventing you from getting in touch with your true nature. In the east, it is the cutting away of old relationships that prohibit your growth. In the south, it is the pruning of your branches to get the best results from your most solid aspects. In the west, the scissors cut away that which is no longer useful in your life and will leave you with only the barren earth in which to plough and plant new seeds to rejuvenate your life.

Sea horses: The sea horse addresses the inner fluidity of family uniting that which gets lost in the depths of extraneous matters. In the north, the sea horse guards the real love and bonds of the family members. In the east, the sea horse whispers of the bonds to each member and asks the sun to join her in resolving family disharmony. In the south, the seahorse gallops in the warmer waters of family abundance and wraps her secret web of energy around the fruitful family. In the west, the sea horse prepares herself to swim to the inner depths of each member of the family to call them back to each other and to the great earth and sea, the birth places of life. This will call a family back to the source of its life and strength.

Shepherd's staff: The shepherd's staff represents the guide that keeps you on the straight and narrow path. It prevents you from going astray during a difficult period. The staff draws energy from above and below and joins them with your energy. In the north, the staff draws the energy of the ancient ones to you for guidance. In the east, it draws the energy of beginning to help you get started. In the south it helps you to draw the energy you need to bring what you are doing into the great light and in the west it will reunite you with the past so that you can travel the descent with grace and peace in knowing that you are guided and protected by the great guardians of the towers.

Shield: The shield protects you from the harsh energy that may come to test your will. If you are weak in your endeavour then your shield will not hold. This

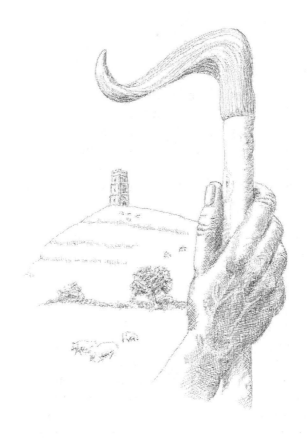

symbol tells you to be sure before you act whenever this may occur.

Shovel: This symbol tells you to break new ground. A shovel means that the time is right to go ahead. It usually involves business or job related plans. The season of the year that this symbol falls in will give you a hint as to when the likelihood of the time will be right. The east is the most advantageous with the north being the least.

Shoe: A shoe represents the need to increase your efforts if you are to succeed and move ahead. This is usually pertinent to relationships. In the east, the shoe means the chance to bring new life into a sagging relationship. In the south, it means that the fruits of the relationship are yours for the taking if you will make the effort. In the west, the cementing of a life long relationship is in the offing for the effort and the north is the joining of soul mates for the effort in asking.

Sickle: This is the harvest, the symbol of reaping. In the north is the security in knowing that what you have prepared for will begin to take root in the coming months. In the east it represents the cash of new ideas is bountiful, and in the south, the ability to move from one project to another and balance the efforts will be fruitful. In the west, the sickle means that you have acted well and you will find much at your feet.

Skull: In some of the older belief systems it was thought that the soul dwelt in the head. If the skull appears in your cup, it is asking you to stop rushing about the material world and spend a little time inside your head, inside your self and do a little spiritual housekeeping. If this appears in your cup keep a live basil plant near your bed for several weeks, this will aid you in this endeavour.

Sled: This is a warning sign and you would be wise to heed it. It tells you that you are on a downhill slide and that the turning point is at hand. If you do not change the course you are on you could find your self needing to completely rethink your life style. In the north, you may be approaching a possible wrong turn so look carefully at which direction you choose to go in. In the east, the sun or the bright light of temporary good fortune may blind you to what may lie underneath. In the south, the prudent person would see that there is much to be lost by inappropriate action and have a period of stillness. In the west, the sled represents the time for bringing a situation to light which is a losing its potential at an ever increasing rate. In this situation, it is better to be wise and look around you with great care.

Snake: Unfortunately the snake represents someone who you think is close to you being untrue. In the north, the snake represents the other person having ideas that, if not put to a halt, will put them into action. In the east, the innocence of your belief in this other person will prevent you at first from being a good observer. In the south, the snake tells you to be careful as you bring your plans to fruition as you may be stung by the ambition of the other persons involved. In the west the snake lies in wait for the unsuspecting. The snake in the west tells you that forewarned is forearmed and that if you have kept yourself to the correct ways of things, the efforts by others will have no effect.

Spear: The spear symbol represents something pierced. Look around the symbol for a clue as to what it is that may be pierced. If it is near a heart shape then it could foretell a broken heart, if on the other hand it is near something that you are having a hard time making headway with it will mean that you will finally break through and make strong headway. You may want to make a mental note of all the symbols around it and ponder its inner meaning.

Spider: The spider is the weaving or the pulling together of the intricate fibres of our lives. The spider indicates that your life is progressing as it should and you should trust in the universe to do its work. In the north, there are new stages of your life being woven for you to experience. In the east, the new fibres, your new accomplishments will shimmer in the light and be an inspiration to continue on. In the south, the spider tells you that you are at your best and that the magnificent fabric of your life should excite you. In the west, it is the time to stand back and look at your web, look at the intricacies that make you unique and celebrate them. They are the magic that makes you a unique person.

Spool: Just as thread is wound around a spool, so our lives spiral around an inner core, the ethos. We become tightly wrapped and it is often difficult to remember that underneath the thread, or the experiences in our lives, lay our true self. In the north, the thread wrapping is begun and we should look for the secrets that are in the world around us. Look for that which you resonate with and go with that. In the east, the threads continue to be wound, be selective as they will be important to you later on, they are integral to the cloth of your life so make them count. In the south, the spool means that it will be filled and that your life will be full and well enjoyed. In the west, you can now use these threads to take stock of the kind of life you are living and whether you may want to make some changes in the time yet to come.

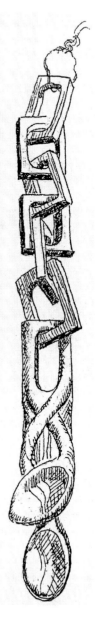

Spoon: A spoon is the symbol of home and hearth. In many cultures, a spoon is hung on the door or fireplace. Spoons can be given as love tokens indicating the intention to set up a home. In the north, the spoon is the possibility of moving house or setting up of a new one. If you are not married, it could be an engagement in the offing. In the east, the spoon is like spring-cleaning, you rearrange the matters in your domestic life and give them a new boost. In the south, the spoon is increase and abundance in your home and the warmth and comfort of your family. In the west, the spoon represents a time to look back on the love and comfort your home has meant and if there are any gaps you can make a list of improvements you want to make in the next season.

Squirrel: the squirrel tells you it is time to set up store. You need to hold on to what is yours as you may at some point face a period of lesser resources. It tells you to be prudent in your affairs and find moderation. A squirrel scampers about the earth gathering in and preparing. Wherever this creature appears in your cup, look at the symbols near by and it will tell you what you are preparing for.

Stairs: This is a symbol that you will succeed. Other polarities or other issues in the cup do not influence it. In the north, the stairs tell you to wait for a time and all things will come in due course. In the east, the success will begin a whole new chapter in your life and leave behind a life that did not work any more. In the south, the stairs tell you that this accomplishment will lead to all the goals you have set for yourself in life. In the west, the stairs tell you of a completed and successful life. Make sure that this success is not at the exclusion of the more important things in life or when you end up in the rest of your life, you may find a serious lacking.

Star: A star is your guide. It is there to light your path by night. When you can see what is in front of you the decisions are there to be made but when you can't see because the secrets are hidden then the star will illuminate those aspects and help you to make the right choice.

Sun: The sun is the god of the heavens and the consort of the mother earth. He warms the earth and stirs the life within to come forth. The sun for you is the same. In the north, the midnight of time, the sun sleeps within the belly of the mother earth and is waiting for the earth to turn. So must you. In the east, the sun stirs and rises and casts rays of gold upon the land and the warmth begins. In the south, the sun is overhead and looks down and caresses all that is on earth. The warmth even reached the depths below the surface and encourages them. In the west, the sun is beginning to sink back into the mother earth and the light fades. Therefore, this is the time for you to stand back and take rest.

Table: The table represents honesty. Putting everything out in the open. It is best to heed this symbol and make sure that there is nothing that you are hiding where you should not. Honestly is always best as living with mis- or half-truth will topple the best built house. In the north, the table tells you to set out as you mean to continue. In the east, it tells you to be sure and up front in everything that you do, even if it means being less grand than you anticipated. In the south, the table tells you that there is bounty to come if you have been honest in your dealings. In the west, the table will be full of your honest efforts and you will

sleep a peaceful rest as a result.

Teapot: Hospitality. A teapot tells you to be a good neighbour. In the north, it means that there may be someone you do not know yet who will need your friendship. In the east, it tells you it is time to go and knock on a door that you haven't yet and offer a cup of friendship. In the south, the teapot tells you that by being a good friend and neighbour that you will never be a lonely person. In the west, the teapot tells you to gather friends and family and enjoy the gathering of love and happiness in your life.

Torch: A torch is telling you that someone will need you to light the way for him or her. When you get the torch in your cup your help will be called for. In the north, you will be asked to help in some sort of planning. In the east, there will be help required getting something off the ground. In the south, the help will be needed to finish a project and in the west to bring in the results. Be careful with this symbol that you do not get taken advantage of and end up doing what you are not comfortable with doing. This can be a good opportunity for you to do a kindness but only when it is on your terms.

Tree: The tree is the Goddesses symbol of so above so below. From her roots, anchored far into the earth the tree sends her trunk and branches reaching for the heavens and the sun. She waves and drinks the whispers of the wind, or its rain and lashing. She

drinks the waters and feels the longing for life. Yet, she is stationary and occupies her space with dignity. She makes of it everything that she possibly can as that is a life's work. The tree tells you to know the ground beneath your feet first before busying yourself with the affairs of beliefs of another.

Triangle: This symbol represents a spiritual awakening or experience. It tells you that you will become aware of the other side of yourself but in a religious sort of way. You will finally solidify your believe or come to understand and know one which may resonate better with who you are. In the north, the time is coming at hand. In the east, the awakening and the realisation of your belief. In the south, the realisation of life for itself and how that plays a part in your own existence will come to you. In the west, you will finally understand within your own heart where the cycle of the web of life fits for you.

Trunk: The trunk, as in storage container, represents your memories, things that you treasure. Your memories are those things that you can take out of your trunk and enjoy forever. In the scope of your life, they are probably the most important treasure. In the north, lay your plans wisely and think about what they would mean as a memory. In the east, pleasant memories of earlier times can add a sweet and lighter dimension to your life, so take time to think on them. In the south, the memories of the times of togetherness and gatherings will fill lonely times. These are the memories that will remind you that life may not be quite so empty as it can often feel. In the west, the trunk is either full or rather empty. It is up to you to decide and act accordingly every day of your life. Do you want happy loving memories or those of days of meaningless tasks?

Turtle: The turtle is sure and steady. He methodically plods ahead and takes time to be observant. He has a hard shell but is very soft underneath and this tells us that we must be able to ward off that which comes to do us harm, but not so hard that we forget to enjoy the poetry of life. The turtle tells you to slow up where ever he lands in your cup and enjoy that season's merit.

Vessel: A vessel is the feelings of a secret admirer. It carries the feelings yet to be born into this life. These feelings are held protected until you notice that the cork is still set in place and make the decision to open the vessel. Make sure that you think wisely as it is an offence to the universe to play with another's feelings if you do not truly want them. In the north, the initiation lies at hand and you must decide when the time is at hand. In the east, let the light of day pour warmth into your heart and take due consideration of the vessel's contents. In the south, it is time to free the contents and take them unto your self, freely taken as freely given. In the west, this means that you have passed by an opportunity to know someone better and that there may still be time if you act swiftly.

Vine: Is the increase in family. The new vine puts out its shoots and clings onto the tree and so balance. It fills with fruit and then the fruit drops to the ground and the seed will grow new vines in the next season. This tells you to remember that as you sew you reap. If the vine continues through more than one season in your cup then you will enjoy new seasons of growth and prosperity for a good long time in the future.

Water: Water is a life element. It is that which allows our lives to flow forward. In the north, the waters have carried that which has laid down in the west into the time before beginning for a rest before beginning life anew. This is the same for you. Your last cycle has been carried to a place where it needs time to recover and rejuvenate. DO NOTHING but dream or lay plans for the future. In the east, the waters are the birthplace of that which is to come. It will carry new life forward and nourish it. In the south, the waters, provide a drink when the heat is above you. Take time out and seek the waters and put your heavy burdens into it, you will see that the waters will carry them away for you. In the west, which is the season of the water, the fluidity between both worlds will allow both your physical side and your spiritual side to be your guide.

Wheel: The wheel represents turning, as all things will do in their own correct time. The wheel tells you that just because you have your own time schedule for things it may not be the correct one or the one for universal ordering. Be patient and let the earth and the universe turn as it will.

It is also telling you that you will need to wait until the season in their cycling change for the next phase to begin and if you push things you will upset a correct order. This would be to a distinct disadvantage for you.

Wishbone: We all think that a wishbone is representative of is decisive luck. In fact, it is the intact wishbone that is important. If you have one it will keep out unwanted intruders. What it actually does is to psychically warn the intruder that if they try and bring harm upon you they too could meet with such fate as this chicken. As such it is a deterrent and will more than likely help protect you. If you bless the creature that gave his bones for this gift, the chances are that that essence will help as a protection mechanism and will bring good fortune to you.

Wolf: The wolf is the protector of the wild forces, those forces that are an intrinsic part of our life and our connection to that which lives by the natural course. The wolf in the north is protecting your nature and that which is in you as you are about to be reborn. In the east, the wolf protects that which is being born and is feeling the light in the innocence of its being. In the south, the wolf protects and will devour that which is not protected so make sure that you do not leave yourself vulnerable. Ask the wolf for insight into where you may lie vulnerable. In the west, the wolf takes unto herself the dying light and is seen fighting against it demanding every breath out of life.

Wreath: The wreath is the eternal circle and tells you that energy, life and love will circle you in your life and you can use it in times of disenchantment. The wreath of light encircles your head and so when this appears in your cup call upon your wisdom to be your guide.

Once you have familiarised yourself with the meanings of each of the symbols you will begin to understand how two or three grouped together may be giving you a message. If you are confused about any of the meanings of their connections to one another, then write down the meanings on a piece of paper and add the meanings together. You may need to close your eyes and just let the ideas and connections come to you slowly as you ponder upon them. Being quiet and calm is the secret to a good reading. Do not force interpretations to come as they are not invoked in that

way. You do not need to force them, be open to them
and let them come to you.

Blessed be - bendith arnom

FREE DETAILED CATALOGUE

Capall Bann is owned and run by people actively involved in many of the areas in which we publish. A detailed illustrated catalogue is available on request, SAE or International Postal Coupon appreciated. **Titles can be ordered direct from Capall Bann, post free in the UK** (cheque or PO with order) or from good bookshops and specialist outlets.

A Breath Behind Time, Terri Hector
Angels and Goddesses - Celtic Christianity & Paganism, M. Howard
Arthur - The Legend Unveiled, C Johnson & E Lung
Astrology The Inner Eye - A Guide in Everyday Language, E Smith
Auguries and Omens - The Magical Lore of Birds, Yvonne Aburrow
Asyniur - Womens Mysteries in the Northern Tradition, S McGrath
Beginnings - Geomancy, Builder's Rites & Electional Astrology in the
        European Tradition, Nigel Pennick
Between Earth and Sky, Julia Day
Book of the Veil , Peter Paddon
Caer Sidhe - Celtic Astrology and Astronomy, Michael Bayley
Call of the Horned Piper, Nigel Jackson
Cat's Company, Ann Walker
Celtic Faery Shamanism, Catrin James
Celtic Lore & Druidic Ritual, Rhiannon Ryall
Celtic Sacrifice - Pre Christian Ritual & Religion, Marion Pearce
Celtic Saints and the Glastonbury Zodiac, Mary Caine
Circle and the Square, Jack Gale
Compleat Vampyre - The Vampyre Shaman, Nigel Jackson
Cottage Witchcraft, Jan McDonald
Creating Form From the Mist - The Wisdom of Women in Celtic Myth and
        Culture, Lynne Sinclair-Wood
Crystal Clear - A Guide to Quartz Crystal, Jennifer Dent
Crystal Doorways, Simon & Sue Lilly
Crossing the Borderlines - Guising, Masking & Ritual Animal Disguise in the
        European Tradition, Nigel Pennick
Dragons of the West, Nigel Pennick
Earth Dance - A Year of Pagan Rituals, Jan Brodie
Earth Harmony - Places of Power, Holiness & Healing, Nigel Pennick
Earth Magic, Margaret McArthur
Eildon Tree (The) Romany Language & Lore, Michael Hoadley
Enchanted Forest - The Magical Lore of Trees, Yvonne Aburrow
Eternal Priestess, Sage Weston

Everything You Always Wanted To Know About Your Body, But So Far
Nobody's Been Able To Tell You, Chris Thomas & D Baker
Face of the Deep - Healing Body & Soul, Penny Allen
Fairies in the Irish Tradition, Molly Gowen
Familiars - Animal Powers of Britain, Anna Franklin
Forest Paths - Tree Divination, Brian Harrison, Ill. S. Rouse
God Year, The, Nigel Pennick & Helen Field
Goddess on the Cross, Dr George Young
Goddess Year, The, Nigel Pennick & Helen Field
Goddesses, Guardians & Groves, Jack Gale
Handbook For Pagan Healers, Liz Joan
Handbook of Fairies, Ronan Coghlan
Healing Book, The, Chris Thomas and Diane Baker
Healing Homes, Jennifer Dent
Healing Journeys, Paul Williamson
Healing Stones, Sue Philips
HerbCraft - Shamanic & Ritual Use of Herbs, Lavender & Franklin
In Search of Herne the Hunter, Eric Fitch
Inner Space Workbook - Develop Thru Tarot, C Summers & J Vayne
Language of the Psycards, Berenice
Legend of Robin Hood, The, Richard Rutherford-Moore
Lid Off the Cauldron, Patricia Crowther
Light From the Shadows - Modern Traditional Witchcraft, Gwyn
Lore of the Sacred Horse, Marion Davies
Magic of Herbs - A Complete Home Herbal, Rhiannon Ryall
Magical Guardians - Exploring the Spirit and Nature of Trees, Philip Heselton
Magical History of the Horse, Janet Farrar & Virginia Russell
Magical Lore of Animals, Yvonne Aburrow
Magical Lore of Cats, Marion Davies
Magical Lore of Herbs, Marion Davies
Magick Without Peers, Ariadne Rainbird & David Rankine
Masks of Misrule - Horned God & His Cult in Europe, Nigel Jackson
Mirrors of Magic - Evoking the Spirit of the Dewponds, P Heselton
Moon Mysteries, Jan Brodie
Mysteries of the Runes, Michael Howard
Mystic Life of Animals, Ann Walker
New Celtic Oracle The, Nigel Pennick & Nigel Jackson
Pagan Feasts - Seasonal Food for the 8 Festivals, Franklin & Phillips
Patchwork of Magic - Living in a Pagan World, Julia Day
Pathworking - A Practical Book of Guided Meditations, Pete Jennings
Personal Power, Anna Franklin
Pickingill Papers - The Origins of Gardnerian Wicca, Bill Liddell
Pillars of Tubal Cain, Nigel Jackson
Places of Pilgrimage and Healing, Adrian Cooper
Practical Divining, Richard Foord
Practical Meditation, Steve Hounsome

Practical Spirituality, Steve Hounsome
Psychic Self Defence - Real Solutions, Jan Brodie
Real Fairies, David Tame
Reality - How It Works & Why It Mostly Doesn't, Rik Dent
Romany Tapestry, Michael Houghton
Runic Astrology, Nigel Pennick
Sacred Animals, Gordon MacLellan
Sacred Celtic Animals, Marion Davies, Ill. Simon Rouse
Sacred Dorset - On the Path of the Dragon, Peter Knight
Sacred Grove - The Mysteries of the Forest, Yvonne Aburrow
Sacred Geometry, Nigel Pennick
Sacred Ring - Pagan Origins of British Folk Festivals, M. Howard
Season of Sorcery - On Becoming a Wisewoman, Poppy Palin
Seasonal Magic - Diary of a Village Witch, Paddy Slade
Secret Places of the Goddess, Philip Heselton
Secret Signs & Sigils, Nigel Pennick
Spirits of the Earth series, Jaq D Hawkins
Stony Gaze, Investigating Celtic Heads John Billingsley
Subterranean Kingdom, The, revised 2nd ed, Nigel Pennick
Talking to the Earth, Gordon MacLellan
Teachings of the Wisewomen, Rhiannon Ryall
Tree: Essence series, Simon & Sue Lilly
Understanding Chaos Magic, Jaq D Hawkins
Warriors at the Edge of Time, Jan Fry
Water Witches, Tony Steele
Way of the Magus, Michael Howard
Weaving a Web of Magic, Rhiannon Ryall
West Country Wicca, Rhiannon Ryall
Wildwitch - The Craft of the Natural Psychic, Poppy Palin
Wildwood King , Philip Kane
Witches of Oz, Matthew & Julia Philips
Wondrous Land - The Faery Faith of Ireland by Dr Kay Mullin
Working With the Merlin, Geoff Hughes

FREE detailed catalogue and FREE 'Inspiration' magazine

Contact: Capall Bann Publishing, Auton Farm, Milverton, Somerset, TA4 1NE

122